ROYAL COURT

Royal Court Theatre presents

uth
nd
conciliation

ebbie tucker green

Theatre

Bloon

nsor Coutts

truth and reconciliation

by debbie tucker green

South African Nana **Cecilia Noble**
South African Mama **Pamela Nomvete**
South African Sister (16) **Vanessa Babirye**
South African Son (15) **Fiston Barek**
South African Daughter, dead (14) **Susan Wokoma**
South African Officer, white **Chris Reilly**

Rwandan Grandfather (Tutsi) **Louis Mahoney**
Rwandan Widow, Stella (Tutsi) **Wunmi Mosaku**
Rwandan Brother (Tutsi) **Ashley Zhangazha**
Rwandan Man (Hutu) **Ivanno Jeremiah**
Rwandan Husband, Moses, dead (Tutsi) **Richie Campbell**

Serbian Man 1 **Aliash Tepina**
Serbian Man 2 **Aleksandar Mikic**
Bosnian Woman **Izabella Urbanowicz**
Bosnian Woman's Friend, female **Wanda Opalinska**

Zimbabwean Husband **Don Gilét**
Zimbabwean Wife **Petra Letang**
Zimbabwean Woman **Sarah Niles**

Northern Irish Woman **Clare Cathcart**
Northern Irish Woman A **Joyce Greenaway**
Northern Irish Man A, Shane **Colm Gormley**
Northern Irish Man B **Ruairi Conaghan**

Director **debbie tucker green**
Designer **Lisa Marie Hall**
Lighting Designer **Matt Haskins**
Sound Designer **Gareth Fry**
Casting Director **Amy Ball**
Assistant Director **Monique Sterling**
Production Manager **Tariq Rifaat**
Trainee Production Manager **Alexandria Stamp**
Stage Managers **Charlotte Padgham, Bryan Paterson**
Costume Supervisors **Iona Kenrick, Amita Kilumanga**
Dialect Coach **Michaela Kennen**
Dialect Assistant **Rachel Coffey**
Movement **Sarah Gorman**
Set Built by **Object Construction Ltd**
Scenic Work by **Jodie Pritchard**

The Royal Court and Stage Management wish to thank the following for their help with this production: Donmar Warehouse, English Touring Theatre, Opera Holland Park, National Theatre.

DEBBIE TUCKER GREEN (Writer & Director)

FOR THE ROYAL COURT: random (& UK tour), stoning mary.

OTHER THEATRE INCLUDES: generations (Young Vic); trade (RSC at Soho); born bad (Hampstead); dirty butterfly (Soho).

TELEVISION & FILM: random, heat (short film), spoil.

RADIO INCLUDES: gone, random, handprint, to swallow, freefall.

DIRECTING INCLUDES: random (film), heat (short film), gone, random (radio).

AWARDS: Olivier Award 'Most Promising Newcomer' for born bad (Hampstead, 2004), OBIE 'Special Citation' for born bad (Soho Rep production, New York 2011).

VANESSA BABIRYE (South African Sister)

FOR THE ROYAL COURT: Vanessa trained at the Identity Drama School. She is making her professional stage debut in truth & reconciliation.

TELEVISION & FILM INCLUDES: Strawberry Fields, random.

FISTON BAREK (South African Son)

THEATRE INCLUDES: Little Baby Jesus (Oval House); Love The Sinner (National).

TELEVISION: Doctors.

RICHIE CAMPBELL (Rwandan Husband, Moses)

FOR THE ROYAL COURT: 93.2FM.

OTHER THEATRE INCLUDES: Lower Ninth (Donmar); The Ones That Flutter (Theatre503); Monster Under the Bed (Polka); Dirty Butterfly (Young Vic); How To Steal a Diamond (Vox Motus/Tron, Glasgow); 3 Days in July (Soho); Little Sweet Thing (Wolsey Theatre, Ipswich/Nottingham Playhouse/Birmingham Rep); Cutter (Half Moon/Lyric Hammersmith); SlamDunk (Tour); Aida (Royal Opera House); This Island's Mine (Millfield Theatre); Eugene Onegin (Royal Opera House).

FILM & TELEVISION INCLUDES: Top Boy, random, Anuvahood, Victim, Game Over, Yesterday's Tomorrow, The Silence, The Firm, Minder, Holby City, And Kill Them, The Bill, Wilderness, The Plague, The Rulers, Dealers and Losers, Just the Two of Us, Babyfathers, Have A Go Heroes.

RADIO: Gone, random, I Fought the Law, 4/4/68.

CLARE CATHCART (Northern Irish Woman)

THEATRE INCLUDES: Our Private Life, Loyal Women.

OTHER THEATRE INCLUDES: The Indian Boys (RSC); Aristocrats (Chichester Festival Theatre); Gone to LA (Hampstead); Sitcom Festival (Riverside Studios); Romeo and Juliet (Greenwich Theatre); After the Rain (Gate); The Party's Over (Nottingham Playhouse); Translations (Donmar); Fooling About (Oxford Stage Co.); Cloud Nine, Duchess of Malfi (Contact Theatre); The Crucible (National).

TELEVISION INCLUDES: Tracey Beaker Returns, The Little House, Ladies of Letters, Beautiful People, Cast Offs, Afterlife, Ultimate Force, Gimme Gimme Gimme, Attachments, Sins, I Saw You, Psychos, Sunny Ears, Accused, Kiss and Tell, Coronation Street, Safe and Sound, The Bill, Casualty, Over Here, Searching, Father Ted, Goodnight Sweetheart, Paris.

FILM INCLUDES: Feast of the Goat, Cor Blimey, Breathtaking, Secret Society, Hotel Splendide, Up on the Roof, Salvage, Amazing Grace.

RADIO INCLUDES: The Other Man, Goya, A Country Dance, Law of Diminishing Returns, The Lights, Angel, Nun Climbs Tree, Le Celestina, Eamon Older Brother of Jesus, We Know Everything, Silver's City.

RUAIRI CONAGHAN (Northern Irish Man B)

FOR THE ROYAL COURT: Trust.

THEATRE INCLUDES: The Crucible, Tearing the Loom, A Midsummer Night's Dream (Lyric, Belfast); I Like Mine with a Kiss (Bush); The Factory Girls (Arcola); A Thousand Yards (Southwark Playhouse); Port Authority, Othello, School for Scandal, The White Devil, Fall From Grace (Liverpool Everyman); Someone to Watch Over Me (Northampton); Scenes from the Big Picture, Peer Gynt (National); Philadelphi Here I Come (Belfast & US Tour).

TELEVISION INCLUDES: The Suspicions of Mr Whicher, Supergrass, Waking the Dead, The Bill, Frances Tuesday, Murphy's Law, Do The Right Thing, All Things Bright and Beautiful, Made in Heaven, Cuchullain.

FILM INCLUDES: It's a Goat's Life, The Catherine Tate Show, An Officer from France, Walk with Me.

RADIO: The Man From God Know's Where, The Lonely Passion of Judith Hearne.

GARETH FRY (Sound Designer)

FOR THE ROYAL COURT: Chicken Soup with Barley, Wastwater, Sucker Punch, The City, O Go My Man (with Out of Joint); Talking to Terrorists (with Out of Joint); Harvest, Forty Winks, Under the Whaleback, Night Songs, Face to the Wall, Redundant, Mountain Language/Ashes to Ashes, The Country.

OTHER THEATRE INCLUDES: Black Watch, Peter Pan, Be Near Me (National Theatre of Scotland); Joe Turner's Come and Gone, Sweet Nothings, The Jewish Wife (Young Vic); Babel (Stan Won't Dance); No Idea (Improbable); The Prisoner of 2nd Avenue (Vaudeville Theatre); Light Shining in Buckinghamshire (Arcola); Fraulein Julie (Schabühne, Berlin); The Duchess of Malfi (Northampton); Beauty and the Beast (Cottesloe Theatre); Endgame, Shun-kin (Complicité); Noise of Time (Complicité with the Emerson String Quartet); Othello (Frantic Assembly); The Fahrenheit Twins (Told By An Idiot); Tangle, Zero Degrees and Drifting (Unlimited Theatre); Astronaut (Theatre O); The Bull, The Flowerbed, Giselle (Fabulous Beast Dance Theatre at the Barbican); Living Costs (DV8 at Tate Modern); After Dido (ENO); Dancing at Lughnasa (Old Vic); Shadowmouth, Romans in Britain (Sheffield Crucible); Phaedra's Love (Bristol Old Vic & Barbican); The Watery Part of the World (Sound & Fury, BAC & UK Tour); The Cat in the Hat, Pains of Youth, Some Trace Of Her, Fram, Women of Troy, Attempts on Her Life, Waves, The Overwhelming, Fix Up, Iphigenia at Aulis, The Three Sisters, Ivanov, The Oresteia (National); A Matter Of Life and Death (Kneehigh/National); Theatre of Blood (Improbable/National); The Overwhelming (Laura Pels Theatre, NY); Macbeth (Out of Joint).

RADIO INCLUDES: Jump, OK Computer, The Overwhelming.

EVENTS INCLUDE: Somerset House Film4 Summer Screen & Ice Rink, Pixar's The Big Cheese Tour.

AWARDS INCLUDE: Laurence Olivier Award 2007 for Waves; Helpmann Award 2008 for Black Watch; Olivier Award 2009 for Black Watch.

DON GILÉT (Zimbabwean Husband)

FOR THE ROYAL COURT: Bone.

OTHER THEATRE INCLUDES: Fabulation (Tricycle); Come out Eli (Arcola); As You Like It (National); Unfinished Business (Talawa); The Alchemist (Present Moment).

TELEVISION INCLUDES: Eastenders, Hotel Babylon, Cape Wrath, Dr Who, Ruby in the Smoke, The Line of Beauty, 55 Degrees North, Silent Witness, Baby Father, Single Voices, Time Gentlemen Please, Cutting It, Brothers and Sisters, Punt and Dennis, Casualty, Now What!, DMOB, Desmonds, Wiz Bang.

FILM INCLUDES: The Wonderland Experience, Greasy, Home Run.

RADIO INCLUDES: Small Island, Days and Nights in Bedlam, Ink, The Liar, Westway.

COLM GORMLEY (Northern Irish Man A, Shane)

THEATRE INCLUDES: Still, the Blackbird Sings (Project Theatre, Dublin/Playhouse, Derry); Arsenic & Old Lace (Salisbury Playhouse); Twelfth Night (Theatre Royal, York); Death of Long Pig (Finborough); Philadephia Here I Come/Aristocrats (European Tour); I'll Be the Devil, All's Well That Ends Well (RSC); The Boy With the Bomb in his Crisps (Belgrade Theatre, Coventry); The Time Step, Water Harvest (Theatre503); The White Devil, The Resistible Rise of Arturo Ui (Mercury Theatre, Colchester); Smiling Through (The Drill Hall); We The People (Shakespeare's Globe); The Ladies Cage (Royal Exchange).

FILM & TELEVISION INCLUDES: Titanic, River City, The Message, Ultimate Force, Bloody Sunday.

JOYCE GREENAWAY (Northern Irish Woman A)

Joyce was born and bred in Northern Ireland and trained at Drama Studio London.

THEATRE INCLUDES: Shore (Riverside Studios); Erris (Theatre503/Black Box Theatre, Belfast); Tall Tales (Clywd Theatre, Cymru); Twopence To Cross The Mersey (Liverpool Empire).

FILM INCLUDES: Winter Escape, Dreadful Bazaar.

Joyce is currently exploring a radio collaboration with new female Irish poets and composers.

LISA MARIE HALL (Designer)

Lisa is a graduate of the National Film & TV School and works as a Production Designer in film, television drama and commercials. She recently designed the film adaptation of random for Channel 4.

FILM & TELEVISION INCLUDES: Holy Flying Circus, random, This Is England '86, Somers Town, Charlie & The Chocolate Factory.

MATT HASKINS (Lighting Designer)

THEATRE INCLUDES: The Years Between (Royal & Derngate); Dream Story, Mud (Gate); The Man with the Luggage, Glass Mountain (Trestle); Peppa Pig's Party, Peppa Pig's Treasure Hunt (UK Tour/West End); Girls Night Out (UK Tour); Blowing Whistles, Hit Me! (Leicester Square Theatre); Lovely & Misfit (Trafalgar Studios).

OPERA INCLUDES: Turn of the Screw, Cautionary Tales (Opera North); Into the Little Hill (Hamburg Laeiszhalle); La Cenerentola (Malmö Opera); Pelléas et Mélisande, The Sofa, The Departure (Independent Opera - Sadlers Wells); Don Pasquale, The Marriage of Figaro, A House on the Moon, Orfeo, Tolomeo (English Touring Opera); Tobias & the Angel (Young Vic/ETO).

SITE SPECIFIC PROJECTS INCLUDE: Thanks A Million (Blonstein & Associates); Dido Queen of Carthage (Kensington Palace); Sea Tongue (The Shout/De La Warr Pavilion); Encounters (Greenwich & Docklands Festival).

OTHER & ASSOCIATE CREDITS INCLUDE: Grace Jones (Royal Albert Hall/ Wireless Festival/ Art Pop Festival); Shun-kin, A Disappearing Number (Complicite).

IVANNO JEREMIAH (Rwandan Man)

Having attended The BRIT School for Performing Arts Ivanno then went on to train at RADA and graduated in July 2010.

THEATRE INCLUDES: As You Like It (West Yorkshire Playhouse); Julius Caesar (RSC Symposium).

FILM AND TELEVISION INCLUDES: The Veteran, Papadopolous & Sons, Injustice, The Jury II.

AWARDS: 2011 Alan Bates Graduate award in association with The Actors Centre.

PETRA LETANG (Zimbabwean Wife)

FOR THE ROYAL COURT: Breath Boom, Fallout, Escobar Estate.

OTHER THEATRE INCLUDES: Every Coin (Synergy/Soho); Joe Turner's Come and Gone, Generations of the Dead (Young Vic); My Wonderful Day (Off Broadway, New York); Baby Girl/The Miracle, The President of an Empty Room (National); The Weave, How Love is Spelt (Bush); Funny Black Women on the Edge (Hackney Empire); Badnuff (Soho); Beautiful Thing (Nottingham Playhouse); Mules (Clean Break); Local Boy (Hampstead).

TELEVISION INCLUDES: Eastenders, The Bill, The Last Detective, Jonathan Creek, Babyfather.

FILM INCLUDES: Betsy and Leonard, Wondrous Oblivion, A Heart Divided.

LOUIS MAHONEY (Rwandan Grandfather)

THEATRE INCLUDES: Love the Sinner, The Observer (National); Romeo and Juliet, Coriolanus (RSC); Cato Street, generations (Young Vic); Desire (Almeida); As You Like It (Leicester Curve); Murderous Angels, Jesus Christ Superstar (Gaiety, Dublin); The White Devil (Oxford Playhouse); Night and Day (Watford Palace); The Raft, Talking to You (West End).

TELEVISION INCLUDES: Waking the Dead, Natural World, The Clinic, Casualty, Doctor Who, Holby City, Fawlty Towers, One Foot in the Algarve, Miss Marple, London's Burning, Death is Part of the Process, Boon, Bergerac, The Lenny Henry Show, The Fight Against Slavery, The Professionals, Black Silk, Sea of Souls.

FILM INCLUDES: Guns at Batasi, Plague of the Zombies, Cry Freedom, White Mischief, Omen III, A Woman Called Golda, Shooting Fish, Live and Let Die, Wondrous Oblivion, Praise Marx and Pass the Ammunition, Shooting Dogs, Rise and Fall of Idi Amin.

ALEKSANDAR MIKIC (Serbian Man 2)

OTHER THEATRE INCLUDES: The Reporter (National); Petrol Jesus Nightmare No 5 (Traverse, Edinburgh); 5/11, King Lear (Chichester Festival Theatre); Cruel and Tender (Young Vic); Gil (784 Theatre Co./Soho); Britannicus, The Cherry Orchard, Suddenly Last Summer (Citizens' Theatre. Glasgow).

TELEVISION INCLUDES: The Gates, Bound, Casualty, Identity, Survivors, Doctor Who, Not Going Out.

FILM INCLUDES: It's A Free World, Eastern Promises.

WUNMI MOSAKU (Rwandan Widow, Stella)

FOR THE ROYAL COURT: The Vertical Hour.

OTHER THEATRE INCLUDES: Katrina (The Bargehouse, London); Mules (Young Vic); Rough Crossings (Headlong/tour/Hammersmith Lyric); The Great Theatre of the World (Arcola).

TELEVISION INCLUDES: Vera, Body Farm, Stolen, 32 Brinkburn Street, Law & Order, One Night in Emergency, Silent Witness, Father and Son, Moses Jones, The Bill, Never Better.

FILM INCLUDES: Patience, Citadel, I Am Slave, Honeymooner, Womb.

RADIO INCLUDES: Amazing Grace, Bad Faith, Normal & Nat, The Vertical Hour.

AWARDS INCLUDE: 2010 Birmingham Black International Film Festival Best Actress Award for I Am Slave, 2010 BEFFTA Best Actress Award for I Am Slave, Rome Fiction Festival Best Actress in a Miniseries for Moses Jones.

SARAH NILES (Zimbabwean Woman)

Sarah trained at the Capitol School of Television & Theatre (Manchester Metropolitan University).

THEATRE INCLUDES: Slave: A Question of Freedom (Feel Good Theatre Company); The Long Road, (Curve Theatre, Leicester); Mrs Afleck (National); The Bogus Woman (Leicester Haymarket/Adelaide Festival/UK Tour); The Lion The Witch and The Wardrobe, To Kill A Mockingbird (Leicester Haymarket); Legends of the Blues (Bridewell Theatre); Entartete Musik (Danish Tour/London Drill Hall); Low Down High Notes (Red Ladder Theatre Company); Magic Sky, Magic Earth (Pentabus Theatre Company); Soho Story (Young Vic Theatre/UK Tour/European Tour); The Pied Piper (Kaboodle Theatre Productions); Black Love (Black Arts Development Project); The Caucasian Chalk Circle (Manchester Library Theatre).

TELEVISION INCLUDES: Being Human, Thorne, Sleepyhead, Beautiful People, Mister Eleven, Peep Show, Doctor Who, A Touch of Frost.

FILM INCLUDES: Now is Good, Austenland, Gravity, London Boulevard, Happy Go Lucky, Games Men Play.

CECILIA NOBLE (South African Nana)

FOR THE ROYAL COURT: Talking in Tongues, This is A Chair, The Sacred Heart.

OTHER THEATRE INCLUDES: The Recruiting Officer, Henry V, His Dark Materials (National); Vagina Monologues (Arts Theatre); Out of the Fog (Almeida); Yellowan (Hampstead); The Birthday Party (Shared Experience); The Tempest, Philoctetes (Cheek by Jowl); Blues for Mr Charlie (Manchester Royal Exchange); In the Red and Brown Water, Raisin in the Sun (Young Vic); Amen Corner (Bristol Old Vic); Seize The Day, Detaining Justice, Wine in the Wilderness, Water, Pecong, The Piano Lesson, Iced (Tricycle).

TELEVISION INCLUDES: Coming Up, Waking the Dead, Eastenders, Silent Witness, The Bill, Holby City, Storm Damage, Thieftakers, Resnick, Casualty, The Rover, Space Precinct.

FILM INCLUDES: Of Mary, New Year's Day, Native, Mrs Caldicott's Cabbage War.

PAMELA NOMVETE (South African Mama)

FOR THE ROYAL COURT: Now or Later.

OTHER THEATRE INCLUDES: Welcome To Thebes, Racing Daemon, David Hare Trilogy, Fuente Ovejuna (National); Twelfth Night (RSC/West End).

TELEVISION INCLUDES: Lewis, Sometimes In April.

FILM: The Special Relationship, Zulu Love Letter.

AWARDS: 2005 Fespaco Film Festival Best Actress award for Zulu Love Letter.

WANDA OPALINSKA (Bosnian Woman's Friend, female)

THEATRE INCLUDES: The Merry Wives of Windsor (Stafford Gatehouse); Ya'akobi and Liedental (Hampstead); Can We Get Les Dennis? (Soho); Seven Deadly Sins (Young Vic, Genesis project); John Prescott's Get Ready Show (UK tour); Medea (Brockley Jack); Wielka Przygoda Puchatka (Polish Tour); Man's Best Friend (Gilded Balloon, Edinburgh Festival Fringe); Uncle Vanya (UK Tour); News Revue (Canal Café).

TELEVISION INCLUDES: Law & Order, Waterloo Road, Coronation Street, Doctors, The Last Laugh, Footballer's Wives TV, The Sitcom Trials.

FILM INCLUDES: The Best Exotic Marigold Hotel, The Wasteland, A Trivial Pursuit, The Diary of Tommy Crisp, The Pitch.

RADIO INCLUDES: The Verb, The Plot, Faction Paradox.

CHRIS REILLY (South African Officer, white)

THEATRE INCLUDES:.45 (Hampstead).

TV INCLUDES: The Undisclosed, Doctors, Scotland's Killers, Five Daughters, Crash.

FILM: The Roundabout.

MONIQUE STERLING (Assistant Director)

AS ASSISTANT DIRECTOR FOR THE ROYAL COURT: Chicken Soup with Barley, Our Private Life, Tribes, Spur of the Moment.

AS DIRECTOR THEATRE INCLUDES: In the Solitude of Cotton Fields (The Clare, Young Vic); A Certain Child (Michael Frayn Studio); Mystical Awakening Extravaganza (BAC); Tuesday (Soho Studio); Ache (Baron's Court Theatre); Dinner Party (George Wood Theatre).

AS ASSISTANT DIRECTOR, OTHER THEATRE INCLUDES: Young NHS project (The Clare, Young Vic); Troilus and Cressida (Shakespeare's Globe); Tunnel 228 (Punchdrunk/Old Vic/Young Vic); Betting on the Dust Commander (Albany Theatre); The Worth of Thunder (Soho Studio); 2008 Schools Festival (Young Vic).

ALIASH TEPINA (Serbian Man 1)

Aliash trained at Central School of Speech and Drama. He is making his professional stage debut in truth & reconciliation.

TELEVISION INCLUDES: Silent Witness, Law & Order: UK, Holby City, Above Suspicion.

FILM INCLUDES: The Dark Knight Rises, The Hidden Memory of Angela Verde, Skriti Spomin Angele Vode.

IZABELLA URBANOWICZ (Bosnian Woman)

Izabella trained at RADA. She is making her professional stage debut in truth & reconciliation.

TELEVISION INCLUDES: The Crimson Petal and The White, Doctors, Titanic.

RADIO: The Archers.

SUSAN WOKOMA (South African Daughter, dead)

Susan graduated from RADA in 2010.

THEATRE INCLUDES: Powder Monkey (Royal Exchange Theatre, Manchester); Theatre Uncut (Southwark Playhouse).

TELEVISION INCLUDES: Doctors, Holby City, Hotel Trubble (regular), That Summer Day.

ASHLEY ZHANGAZHA (Rwandan Brother)

Ashley trained at Guildhall School of Music and Drama.

THEATRE INCLUDES: King Lear (Donmar/Tour/New York); Danton's Death (National); Oliver, Whistle Down the Wind, Hey Mr Producer (West End); Much Ado About Nothing (NYT).

TELEVISION INCLUDES: Lenny Goes to Town, Axon.

AWARDS: 2011 Ian Charleson Award Commendation for King Lear, 2009 Lilian Baylis Prize.

THE ENGLISH STAGE COMPANY
AT THE ROYAL COURT THEATRE

*'For me the theatre is really a religion or way of life.
You must decide what you feel the world is about
and what you want to say about it, so that everything
in the theatre you work in is saying the same thing
... A theatre must have a recognisable attitude. It will
have one, whether you like it or not.'*

George Devine, first artistic director of the
English Stage Company: notes for an unwritten
book.

photo: Stephen Cummiskey

As Britain's leading national company dedicated to new work, the Royal Court Theatre produces new plays of the highest quality, working with writers from all backgrounds, and asking questions about who we are and the world in which we live.

"The Royal Court has been at the centre of British cultural life for the past 50 years, an engine room for new writing and constantly transforming the theatrical culture." Stephen Daldry

Since its foundation in 1956, the Royal Court has presented premieres by almost every leading contemporary British playwright, from John Osborne's Look Back in Anger to Caryl Churchill's A Number and Tom Stoppard's Rock 'n' Roll. Just some of the other writers to have chosen the Royal Court to premiere their work include Edward Albee, John Arden, Richard Bean, Samuel Beckett, Edward Bond, Leo Butler, Jez Butterworth, Martin Crimp, Ariel Dorfman, Stella Feehily, Christopher Hampton, David Hare, Eugène Ionesco, Ann Jellicoe, Terry Johnson, Sarah Kane, David Mamet, Martin McDonagh, Conor McPherson, Joe Penhall, Lucy Prebble, Mark Ravenhill, Simon Stephens, Wole Soyinka, Polly Stenham, David Storey, Debbie Tucker Green, Arnold Wesker and Roy Williams.

"It is risky to miss a production there." Financial Times

In addition to its full-scale productions, the Royal Court also facilitates international work at a grass roots level, developing exchanges which bring young writers to Britain and sending British writers, actors and directors to work with artists around the world. The research and play development arm of the Royal Court Theatre, The Studio, finds the most exciting and diverse range of new voices in the UK. The Studio runs play-writing groups including the Young Writers Programme, Critical Mass for black, Asian and minority ethnic writers and the biennial Young Writers Festival. For further information, go to http://www.royalcourttheatre.com/playwriting.

"Yes, the Royal Court is on a roll. Yes, Dominic Cooke has just the genius and kick that this venue needs... It's fist-bitingly exciting." Independent

ROYAL COURT SUPPORTERS

The Royal Court is able to offer its unique playwriting and audience development programmes because of significant and longstanding partnerships with the organisations that support it.

Coutts is the Principal Sponsor of the Royal Court. The Genesis Foundation supports the Royal Court's work with International Playwrights. Theatre Local is sponsored by Bloomberg. The Jerwood Charitable Foundation supports new plays by playwrights through the Jerwood New Playwrights series. The Artistic Director's Chair is supported by a lead grant from The Peter Jay Sharp Foundation, contributing to the activities of the Artistic Director's office. Over the past ten years the BBC has supported the Gerald Chapman Fund for directors.

The Harold Pinter Playwright's Award is given annually by his widow, Lady Antonia Fraser, to support a new commission at the Royal Court.

PUBLIC FUNDING
Arts Council England, London
British Council
European Commission Representation in the UK

CHARITABLE DONATIONS
American Friends of the Royal Court
Martin Bowley Charitable Trust
The Brim Foundation*
Gerald Chapman Fund
City Bridge Trust
Cowley Charitable Trust
The H and G de Freitas Charitable Trust
The Dorset Foundation
The John Ellerman Foundation
The Eranda Foundation
Genesis Foundation
J Paul Getty Jnr Charitable Trust
The Golden Bottle Trust
The Haberdashers' Company
Paul Hamlyn Foundation
Jerwood Charitable Foundation
Marina Kleinwort Charitable Trust
The Leathersellers' Company
John Lyon's Charity
The Andrew W Mellon Foundation
The Laura Pels Foundation*
Jerome Robbins Foundation*
Rose Foundation
Royal Victoria Hall Foundation
The Dr Mortimer & Theresa Sackler Foundation
The Peter Jay Sharp Foundation*
The Steel Charitable Trust
John Thaw Foundation
The Garfield Weston Foundation

CORPORATE SUPPORTERS & SPONSORS
BBC
Bloomberg
Coutts
Ecosse Films
French Wines
Grey London
Kudos Film & Television
MAC
Moët & Chandon
Oakley Capital Limited
Sky Arts
Smythson of Bond Street
White Light Ltd

BUSINESS ASSOCIATES, MEMBERS & BENEFACTORS
Auerbach & Steele Opticians
Bank of America Merrill Lynch
Hugo Boss
Lazard
Louis Vuitton
Oberon Books
Savills
Vanity Fair

DEVELOPMENT ADVOCATES
John Ayton
Elizabeth Bandeen
Tim Blythe
Anthony Burton
Sindy Caplan
Sarah Chappatte
Cas Donald (Vice Chair)
Allie Esiri
Celeste Fenichel
Anoushka Healy
Emma Marsh (Chair)
William Russell
Deborah Shaw Marquardt (Vice Chair)
Nick Wheeler
Daniel Winterfeldt

Supported by
ARTS COUNCIL ENGLAND

INDIVIDUAL MEMBERS

ICE-BREAKERS
ACT IV
Anonymous
Mrs Rosemary Alexander
Mr & Mrs Tony Ball
David Barnes
Lisa & Andrew Barnett
Mrs Renate Blackwood
Ossi & Paul Burger
Helena Butler
Leigh & Lena Collins
Mr Claes Hesselgren & Mrs Jane Collins
Mark & Tobey Dichter
Ms P Dolphin
Elizabeth & James Downing
Virginia Finegold
Charlotte & Nick Fraser
Alistair & Lynwen Gibbons
Mark & Rebecca Goldbart
Mr & Mrs Green
Sebastian & Rachel Grigg
Mrs Hattrell
Madeleine Hodgkin
Steven & Candice Hurwitz
Mrs R Jay
David Lanch
Louisa Lane Fox
Yasmine Lever
Colette & Peter Levy
Mr & Mrs Peter Lord
David Marks QC
Nicola McFarland
Jonathan & Edward Mills
Ann Norman-Butler
Emma O'Donoghue
Michael & Janet Orr
Mr & Mrs William Poeton
Mr M Polglase
Really Useful Theatres
Mr & Mrs Tim Reid
Mrs Lois Sieff OBE
Mr & Mrs L Slaughter
Nick & Louise Steidl
Torsten Thiele
Laura & Stephen Zimmerman

GROUND-BREAKERS
Anonymous
Moira Andreae
Simon Andrews
Nick Archdale
Charlotte Asprey
Jane Attias*
Caroline Baker
Brian Balfour-Oatts
Elizabeth & Adam Bandeen
Ray Barrell
Dr Kate Best
Dianne & Michael Bienes
Stan & Val Bond
Kristina Borsy & Nick Turdean
Neil & Sarah Brener
Mrs Deborah Brett
Sindy & Jonathan Caplan
Gavin & Lesley Casey
Sarah & Philippe Chappatte
Tim & Caroline Clark
Carole & Neville Conrad
Kay Ellen Consolver & John Storkerson
Clyde Cooper
Ian & Caroline Cormack
Mr & Mrs Cross
Andrew & Amanda Cryer
Alison Davies
Noel De Keyzer
Polly Devlin OBE
Rob & Cherry Dickins
Denise & Randolph Dumas
Zeina Durra & Saadi Soudavar
Robyn Durie
Glenn & Phyllida Earle
Allie Esiri
Margaret Exley CBE
Celeste & Peter Fenichel
Margy Fenwick
The Edwin Fox Foundation
John Garfield
Beverley Gee
Dina Geha & Eric Lopez
Mr & Mrs Georgiades
Nick & Julie Gould
Lord & Lady Grabiner
Richard & Marcia Grand*
Reade & Elizabeth Griffith
Don & Sue Guiney
Jill Hackel & Andrzej Zarzycki
Mary & Douglas Hampson
Sally Hampton
Jennifer Harper
Sam & Caroline Haubold
Anoushka Healy
Mr & Mrs Johnny Hewett
Gordon Holmes
The David Hyman Charitable Trust
Mrs Madeleine Inkin
Nicholas Jones
Nicholas Josefowitz
Dr Evi Kaplanis
David Kaskel & Christopher Teano
Vincent & Amanda Keaveny
Peter & Maria Kellner*
Nicola Kerr
Philip & Joan Kingsley
Mr & Mrs Pawel Kisielewski
Maria Lam
Larry & Peggy Levy
Daisy & Richard Littler
Kathryn Ludlow
James & Beatrice Lupton
David & Elizabeth Miles
Barbara Minto
Ann & Gavin Neath CBE
Murray North
Clive & Annie Norton
Georgia Oetker
William Plapinger & Cassie Murray*
Andrea & Hilary Ponti
Wendy & Philip Press
Julie Ritter
Mark & Tricia Robinson
Paul & Gill Robinson
William & Hilary Russell
Julie & Bill Ryan
Sally & Anthony Salz
Bhags Sharma
Mrs Doris Sherwood
The Michael & Melanie Sherwood Charitable Foundation
Tom Siebens & Mimi Parsons
Anthony Simpson & Susan Boster
Richard Simpson
Brian Smith
Samantha & Darren Smith
The Ulrich Family
The Ury Trust
Amanda Vail

Matthew & Sian Westerman
Mr & Mrs Nick Wheeler
Carol Woolton
Katherine & Michael Yates*

BOUNDARY-BREAKERS
Katie Bradford
Sir Trevor & Lady Chinn
Mr & Mrs Roderick Jack
Ms Alex Joffe
Steve Kingshott
Emma Marsh
Paul & Jill Ruddock

MOVER-SHAKERS
Anonymous
Mr & Mrs Ayton
Cas Donald
Lloyd & Sarah Dorfman
Lydia & Manfred Gorvy
Duncan Matthews QC
Ian & Carol Sellars
Edgar & Judith Wallner

HISTORY-MAKERS
Eric Abraham & Sigrid Rausing

MAJOR DONORS
Rob & Siri Cope
Daniel & Joanna Friel
Jack & Linda Keenan*
Deborah & Stephen Marquardt
Miles Morland
The David & Elaine Potter Foundation
Lady Sainsbury of Turville
NoraLee & Jon Sedmak*
Jan & Michael Topham
The Williams Charitable Trust

*Supporters of the American Friends of the Royal Court (AFRCT)

FOR THE ROYAL COURT

Royal Court Theatre, Sloane Square, London SW1W 8AS
Tel: 020 7565 5050 Fax: 020 7565 5001
info@royalcourttheatre.com, www.royalcourttheatre.com

Artistic Director **Dominic Cooke**
Associate Directors **Simon Godwin, Jeremy Herrin*,
Sacha Wares***
Artistic Associate **Emily McLaughlin***
Diversity Associate **Ola Animashawun***
Education Associate **Lynne Gagliano***
PA to the Artistic Director **Pamela Wilson**

Literary Manager **Christopher Campbell**
Senior Reader **Nicola Wass****
Literary Assistant **Marcelo Dos Santos**
Studio Administrator **Clare McQuillan**
Writers' Tutor **Leo Butler***
Pearson Playwright **DC Moore ^**

Associate Director International **Elyse Dodgson**
International Projects Manager **Chris James**
International Assistant **William Drew**

Casting Director **Amy Ball**
Casting Assistant **Lotte Hines**

Head of Production **Paul Handley**
JTU Production Manager **Tariq Rifaat**
Production Assistant **Rebecca Maltby**
Head of Lighting **Matt Drury**
Lighting Deputy **Stephen Andrews**
Lighting Assistants **Katie Pitt, Jack Williams**
Lighting Board Operator **Jack Champion**
Head of Stage **Steven Stickler**
Stage Deputy **Dan Lockett**
Stage Chargehand **Lee Crimmen**
Chargehand Carpenter **Richard Martin**
Head of Sound **David McSeveney**
Sound Deputy **Alex Caplen**
Sound Operator **Sam Charleston**
Head of Costume **Iona Kenrick**
Costume Deputy **Jackie Orton**
Wardrobe Assistant **Pam Anson**

Executive Director **Kate Horton**
General Manager **Catherine Thornborrow**
Administrative Assistant **Holly Handel**

Head of Finance & Administration **Helen Perryer**
Senior Finance & Administration Officer
Martin Wheeler
Finance Officer **Rachel Harrison***
Finance & Administration Assistant **Tessa Rivers**

Head of Marketing & Sales **Becky Wootton**
Acting Marketing Manager **Helen Slater**
Press & Public Relations Officer **Anna Evans**
Communications Assistant **Ruth Hawkins**
Communications Interns **Hannah Clapham, Anoushka
Warden**
Sales Manager **Kevin West**
Deputy Sales Manager **Liam Geoghegan**
Box Office Sales Assistants **Joe Hodgson, Carla
Kingham*, Stephen Laughton*, Helen Murray*,
Ciara O'Toole, Helen Preddy***

Head of Development **Gaby Styles**
Senior Development Manager **Hannah Clifford**
Development Managers **Lucy Buxton, Luciana Lawlor**
Development Officer **Penny Saward**
Development Intern **Dean Stigwood**

Theatre Manager **Bobbie Stokes**
Front of House Manager **Rachel Dudley**
Events Manager **Joanna Ostrom**
Duty Managers **Fiona Clift*, Elinor Keber***
Front of House Assistant **Deirdre Lennon***
Bar & Food Manager **Sami Rifaat**
Deputy Bar & Food Manager **Ali Christian**
Interim Head Chef **Tim Jenner**
Sous Chef **Paulino Chuitcheu**
Bookshop Manager **Simon David**
Bookshop Assistants **Vanessa Hammick*, Tom Clancy***
Stage Door/Reception **Paul Lovegrove, Tyrone Lucas**

Thanks to all of our ushers and bar staff.

^This theatre has the support of the Pearson Playwrights'
Scheme sponsored by the Peggy Ramsay Foundation.

** The post of Senior Reader is supported by NoraLee & Jon
Sedmak through the American Friends of the Royal Court
Theatre.

‡The post of the Trainee Director is supported by the BBC
writersroom.

* Part-time.

ENGLISH STAGE COMPANY

President
Dame Joan Plowright CBE

Honorary Council
Sir Richard Eyre CBE
Alan Grieve CBE
Martin Paisner CBE

Council
Chairman **Anthony Burton**
Vice Chairman **Graham Devlin CBE**

Members
Jennette Arnold OBE
Judy Daish
Sir David Green KCMG
Joyce Hytner OBE
Stephen Jeffreys
Wasfi Kani OBE
Phyllida Lloyd CBE
James Midgley
Sophie Okonedo OBE
Alan Rickman
Anita Scott
Katharine Viner
Stewart Wood

Autumn 2011

Jerwood Theatre Downstairs

13 Oct – 19 Nov

jumpy
by April De Angelis

2 Dec – 14 Jan

haunted child
by Joe Penhall

Jerwood Theatre Upstairs

11 Oct – 5 Nov

bang bang bang
by Stella Feehily

Co-production with the Royal Court, Out of Joint,
The Curve, Leicester, The Octagon, Bolton and
Salisbury Playhouse.

25 Nov – 23 Dec

the westbridge
by Rachel De-lahay

020 7565 5000
www.royalcourttheatre.com

truth and reconciliation

debbie tucker green

Characters

SOUTH AFRICAN MUM (MAMA)
S.A. GRANDMA (NANA)
S.A. SON, *fifteen*
S.A. DAUGHTER, *sixteen*
S.A. SISTER (CHILD), *dead, fourteen*
S.A. OFFICER, *white, male*

BOSNIAN WOMAN
BOSNIAN WOMAN'S FEMALE FRIEND
SERBIAN MAN 1, *ex-soldier*
SERBIAN MAN 2, *ex-soldier*

ZIMBABWEAN WIFE
ZIMBABWEAN HUSBAND
ZIMBABWEAN WOMAN

RWANDAN WIDOW (*Stella*), *Tutsi*
RWANDAN BROTHER, *Tutsi, older than widow*
RWANDAN GRANDFATHER, *Tutsi*
RWANDAN MAN, *Hutu, he has a visible scar on him*
RWANDAN HUSBAND OF STELLA (MOSES), *dead, Tutsi*

NORTHERN IRISH WOMAN
NORTHERN IRISH WOMAN A
NORTHERN IRISH MAN A (*Shane*)
NORTHERN IRISH MAN B

Note on the text

The South African family and Zimbabwean characters are Black. Bosnian, Serb, South African Officer and Irish characters are white.

Places and dates should be shown.

Names appearing without dialogue indicate an active silence between those characters.

A forward slash (/) marks where dialogue starts to overlap.

Words in (brackets) are intention only and not to be spoken.

This text went to press before the end of rehearsals and so may differ slightly from the play as performed.

South Africa 1998

Three wooden chairs face one solitary wooden chair.
NANA, MAMA, SON *and* DAUGHTER *watch the empty seats.*
NANA *is not impressed.*

NANA   … Not even a cushion.

NANA slowly sits in one of the three.

The KIDS *take the other two seats. The chair opposite remains empty.*

Not even a soft to soften the seat.
Not a little something to ease my sitting –
leave a seat for your mama –

DAUGHTER *stands.* MAMA *doesn't move.*

let her come and sit and share the harshness of the – (*To* MAMA.) not even a cushion –

SON *stands – looks at his sister.*

SON   Mama you can sit / here.

DAUGHTER   She can sit here –

SON   Mama?

MAMA *stays standing.*

NANA   She needs only one seat so one of you stop standing and sit down.

SON   Mama?

NANA   I do not need –

4

SON	Mama – here – you can sit / here.
	DAUGHTER *re-sits*.
NANA	I do not need to sit here on these harsh seats alone.
DAUGHTER	What if it's a she? …What if it's a / she?
SON	It won't be a / she.
NANA	She needs to sit –
DAUGHTER	it might / be a –
SON	it won't be a / she.
NANA	She needs to sit down by me – standing will stand for nothing.
DAUGHTER	(*To* SON.) You don't know if / it's –
SON	Their women aren't on the front line –
NANA	Standing is not a statement.
DAUGHTER	Theirs might / be.
SON	They don't let their women on their front / line.
NANA	Tell your mama to sit.
	DAUGHTER *gets up again*. MAMA *doesn't move*.
DAUGHTER	Mama. (You can) sit here
NANA	by me
DAUGHTER	by Nana… Here.
	SON *re-sits*.
NANA	A mama next to a mama – a mama next to her mama.

SON	What women of theirs do you know that stand and fight?
DAUGHTER	You don't know about their / women.
SON	Know that their women don't work
DAUGHTER	you / don't know –
SON	know that their women don't have to work, that their women live leisurely, know that their women don't do anything they don't have to – know that their women don't fight. That their women don't have to fight. That their women wait for their men to return and give them kisses and hot tea when they are back and ask about their day but don't ask about their day.
DAUGHTER	
SON	
SON	I don't want to talk about their women. Their women aren't like our women. I don't want to know about / them.
NANA	Tell her let us sit together as mamas.
SON	Mama?

DAUGHTER *doesn't know whether to stay standing or sit, looks between* NANA *and* MAMA, DAUGHTER *sits.*

DAUGHTER	If it is a woman –
SON	it will be a man.
DAUGHTER	But if it is a woman –
SON	it won't be a / woman.
NANA	As the nana –
DAUGHTER	if it's a / woman –

NANA	as her nana
SON	if it is a woman that would be worse.
NANA	As the mama – as her mama…
DAUGHTER	Mama?
NANA	As your mama we should sit. Side by side. In… solidarity. Or something. This hard chair –
DAUGHTER	could it / be a woman?
NANA	on this hard chair –
DAUGHTER	could it be a / woman?
NANA	in this hard place. In this hard place they want to tell me about my granddaughter? Eh? *Tell* your mama to sit down –
DAUGHTER	Mama –
NANA	give her room…

DAUGHTER *stands.*

Give her room so she can sit down on this hard chair… by me.

MAMA *doesn't move.*

Rwanda 2005

	BROTHER *at the end of a cigarette smokes.* ALL *are standing.*
WIDOW	You smoke like you are nervous –
BROTHER	I'm not nervous.
	Beat.
WIDOW	You smoke like you / are (nervous).
BROTHER	I am not nervous
WIDOW	like you are afraid
GRANDDAD	he is not nervous
BROTHER	I have nothing to be afraid of.
	Beat.
WIDOW	I would have come on my own –
BROTHER	you can't drive
GRANDDAD	she can't drive.
WIDOW	I could have come on my own –
GRANDDAD	you couldn't
BROTHER	I wouldn't let you.
WIDOW	You wouldn't 'let' me.
GRANDDAD	*I* wouldn't let you. I wouldn't let him let you.
BROTHER	…I wouldn't want you here on your own.
WIDOW	

8

GRANDDAD	We wanted to come.
BROTHER	
GRANDDAD	

> BROTHER *draws on his cigarette*.
> WIDOW *sees*.

WIDOW	I could have come on / my own.
GRANDDAD	I wanted to come – you would deny me coming? He wanted to come whatever he says and however hard he smokes he wanted to be here.

> BROTHER *has started another cigarette*.

WIDOW	You wanted to / come?

> *He smokes*.

GRANDDAD	He wanted to come. He wanted to drive. He wanted to drive you.
WIDOW	… You smoke like you are nervous.
BROTHER	You can't drive.
WIDOW	I needed to / come.
BROTHER	You can't drive.
GRANDDAD	You are smoking like you are afraid.
BROTHER	I am not afraid. There is nothing to be afraid of.

Bosnia 1996

Two Serb MEN *in civvies (ex-soldiers)*
standing.
They are awkward in each other's
presence.
They are waiting.

Beat.
Beat.

MAN 2 *gets out a pack of cigarettes,*
offers.
MAN 1 *grunts his 'no thanks'.*

MAN 2   Stopped?

MAN 1 *grunts.*
Beat.

You've stopped?

MAN 1   Hm.

Beat.

MAN 2   You've stopped smoking?

Beat.

MAN 1   ... Hm.

Beat.
MAN 2 *watches him a moment.*

MAN 1   Doesn't agree with me.

MAN 2   Doesn't agree with you?

MAN 1   Hm.

Beat.

MAN 2   … Smoking doesn't agree with you.

                … Now.

                Beat.

MAN 1   I just drink.

                Beat.

                A lot.
                A lot of the time.

MAN 2   Hm.

MAN 1   All of the time.

                Beat.
                Beat.

                Light up.

                MAN 2 *doesn't.*

                Light up.

                MAN 2 *doesn't.*
                Beat.

                Don't let me stop you / from –

MAN 2   You couldn't stop me.

MAN 1   … Hmm.

                Beat.

MAN 2   No one said about having to wait. They
                don't tell you this – didn't say about this –
                this is – no one said about (having to) – I'm
                not waiting I'm not waiting long. I've
                things to do other things to do other things I
                should be (doing) –

BOSNIAN WOMAN walks in, they clock her. Her FRIEND follows, but they only watch BOSNIAN WOMAN who is heavily pregnant.

Rwanda 2005

GRANDDAD, WIDOW *and* BROTHER
slowly take to three wooden seats. They are
nervous. BROTHER *seats* GRANDDAD,
seats WIDOW, *before slowly taking a seat*
himself.
They wait.
There is one empty seat left, opposite them.

Beat.

A MAN (*Hutu*) *enters. Something tired*
about him.
Their eyes never leave him.

He takes his seat opposite them – WIDOW
tries to hold herself together, but lets out a
small gasp.

Zimbabwe 2007

In a modest room in a modest house. The
Black ZIMBABWEAN HUSBAND *and*
WIFE *sit and wait.*
They try to talk quietly.

Pause.

HUSBAND   … I can't protect you.

WIFE

HUSBAND   I can't protect / you.

WIFE   I never asked you / to.

HUSBAND   Not against this.

WIFE   I'm not asking for you to / protect (me).

HUSBAND   Not asking that of me either?

Beat.

WIFE   I don't expect –

HUSBAND   I do.
I want to – you should want me to – you'll
need me to – you should need me / to –

WIFE   I –

HUSBAND   but. I… I can't.

Beat.

WIFE   I didn't want you to change my mind.

HUSBAND   … If your mind was there to change –

WIFE   I didn't want you to change my / mind.

HUSBAND	If your mind was there to change then you weren't sure and if you weren't sure – aren't sure – then you should have said. Nothing.
WIFE	I am / sure.
HUSBAND	Say 'nothing'. Not 'anything' – not 'something'. Let your unsure mind – tell your unsure mouth to surely be quiet. … Telling the world first and me / later.
WIFE	It wasn't 'the world' – it was just / a –
HUSBAND	you didn't tell / me
WIFE	just a few
HUSBAND	'a few'?
WIFE	A few.
HUSBAND	A 'few' of who?
WIFE	A few others.
HUSBAND	… A few is enough.
HUSBAND WIFE	
HUSBAND	If it had to be said –
WIFE	it was ready to be said.
HUSBAND	If it had to be / said –
WIFE	it 'needed' to be said –
HUSBAND	not by you
WIFE	somebody had to speak
HUSBAND	not / you
WIFE	somebody had to say / something

HUSBAND	not you – let someone say it – not you
WIFE	*you* were saying –
HUSBAND	to *you* – not to 'a few' – not to just anybody –
WIFE	they were not 'just anybody' – I don't talk to 'just / anybody' –
HUSBAND	not to 'a few' / of –
WIFE	it was / only –
HUSBAND	not to 'a few' of 'anybody' else.

They wait.

… There are people who say things better
than you.
There are people who have better words
better speaking
better ways of speaking.
There are people paid to say
born to say.
People who don't stop saying things
the right things
at the right time
better than you
surer than you
louder than you
more… effective.

There are people who will be heard
people who will matter
people whose words will matter.
Let them say.
Let *them* speak.
And we will agree with them.
We can agree with them
we do agree with them.
We may even vote for them.

	When we are allowed to. You are my wife –
WIFE	We / can –
HUSBAND	and I love you – but you should have told (me) – you should have told me. First. Before you told your…
	a 'few'.
	Beat. *Beat.*
WIFE	(*Quietly.*) … We can leave this place.
HUSBAND	What?
WIFE	We can leave this place
HUSBAND	we've left one place.
WIFE	We can leave again
HUSBAND	to get to where?
WIFE	
WIFE	We can –
HUSBAND	what?
	Beat.
WIFE	I can –
HUSBAND	what?
WIFE	
WIFE	… You can leave.
HUSBAND WIFE	
HUSBAND	… Without you??

Bosnia 1996

> *The two Serb* MEN (*ex-soldiers*) *in civvies
> on the side of the solo chair. One* MAN *sits,
> the other awkwardly stays standing.* MAN 2
> *clumsily puts out his cigarette.* BOSNIAN
> WOMAN (*and* FRIEND) *seated opposite
> them watches, heavily pregnant.*

> *Beat.*

> BOSNIAN WOMAN *and* FRIEND *talk
> quietly together.* (*Something we don't fully
> hear.*) *After a while they finish.*

> *Beat.*
> *Beat.*

> BOSNIAN WOMAN *looks to her*
> FRIEND, *who indicates for her to speak.*
> *Beat.*

B. WOMAN   (*Quietly. To* FRIEND.) … Are they
expecting me to… (speak?)

Are they waiting for me to speak first?

Beat.

… Does he want me to tell him? Do they
want me to tell them?
… What do they want?

Do *I* need to tell them? Do they need me to
tell / them?

MAN 1   (*Quietly.*) I do not know this / woman.

B. WOMAN   Do *I* have to tell / them?

18

MAN 1	I do not know this / woman.
FRIEND	Tell them.
B. WOMAN	
MAN 1	
FRIEND	Tell them.
MAN 1	I –
B. WOMAN	I came here by bus. Here.

In these flat shoes.
Here.

… I walked the three miles to the stop to
wait for the bus.
To get to… here.

Beat.

(*To* FRIEND.) Is it not for them to speak?

FRIEND	Tell them.
B. WOMAN	Is this what they are waiting for me to say?
FRIEND	Tell / them.
B. WOMAN	But it's for them to speak.
FRIEND	It is for them to speak –
B. WOMAN	for them to say something to / me.
FRIEND	For them to say something to you. Yes. But.
B. WOMAN	Tell them to tell me. Please.
FRIEND	
B. WOMAN	Tell them to speak.

Beat.

MAN 2

B. WOMAN	I waited for over an hour. Standing, then sitting – there was nowhere to sit but I sat. Down. To wait. For the bus.
MAN 1	I do not know / this woman.
B. WOMAN	I sat at a window seat on the bus with a man your age sat by me. And I couldn't return his smile. Wouldn't return his / smile.
MAN 1	I do not / know you.
B. WOMAN	When he asked me where I was going I told him – here.
MAN 1	I don't know / her.
B. WOMAN	When he asked me why I… refused him an answer.
MAN 1	Tell your friend –
FRIEND	no.
MAN 1	Tell –
FRIEND	no.
B. WOMAN	Riding for two hours sat next to someone I could hear wondering. About me. About me – coming / here.
MAN 1	Tell / her.
FRIEND	*No*.
B. WOMAN	I got off at the wrong stop –
FRIEND	You speak –
B. WOMAN	one stop too / early
FRIEND	you speak to her

MAN 1	I / don't –
B. WOMAN	by mistake. And walked the rest. In these flat shoes. To get to… here.
MAN 1	Lady I do not / know you.
B. WOMAN	I am no *lady* now – do you think that I would / come –
MAN 1	tell her I don't know / her
B. WOMAN	come all this / way –
MAN 1	tell your friend that I / don't know her
B. WOMAN	that I would come all this way without being sure that I would know (you)? – You sit there and make me speak first you sit there saying nothing and think that I wouldn't know *you* – *both* of you?

South Africa 1998

> *NANA, SON and DAUGHTER are seated on the three chairs.*
>
> *The empty chair faces them. MAMA still stands.*

NANA
DAUGHTER
SON

> *SON struggles out of his battered jacket, checks the pockets, before passing the jacket to his seated sister, who passes it to NANA.*
> *NANA carefully folds it, wearily stands – places the folded jacket down on her chair, before slowly lowering herself on it.*
>
> *Beat.*

DAUGHTER   Why are they making us wait?
            … Why are they making us wait? Nana, why are they making us wait –

SON   he

DAUGHTER   she

SON   should wait for us – he

DAUGHTER   she

SON   should be sitting waiting for us. Should be made to wait for us – should be told we won't come till he is waiting. He should be sitting on his hard chair – we should come when we like – we should turn up when we

	like – we shouldn't be the ones (waiting) – we shouldn't be waiting for him –
DAUGHTER	or her
SON	to get ready to come to us. They should ask if we are ready – it is for us to be ready – they should wait to respond to our readiness not for us to wait for them.
	Beat.
DAUGHTER	Is that why we're waiting – they're not ready? How can they not be ready? Didn't she know we were going to come?
NANA	They know we are coming.
DAUGHTER	They knew we were coming
SON	why are they making us / wait?
NANA	They know we are here.
	Beat.
DAUGHTER	(*To* SON.) … Do you know what you are going to ask?
SON	
DAUGHTER	Mama what are you going to ask?
MAMA	
DAUGHTER	(*To* NANA.) Do you know what you are going to / say?
SON	Know what I'm going to say –
DAUGHTER	I have a list
SON	I don't need a list.
DAUGHTER	I have a lot to / ask.
SON	I should not have to ask. He will tell us what he / knows.

23

DAUGHTER	If she doesn't, I will / ask –
SON	He will tell us. He will tell us – he will tell / me –
NANA	Tell your mama she needs to / sit.
SON	tell me what he knows. He will sit there –
DAUGHTER	Mama –
SON	and say what he knows to / me
DAUGHTER	Mama –
SON	without me asking twice. I am ready.
DAUGHTER	Mama… Please… Sit down.

Rwanda 2005

> *The* MAN *sits on the solo chair, something tired about him.* WIDOW *sits across from him.* GRANDDAD *and* BROTHER *stand.*

WIDOW
WIDOW
MAN

WIDOW   (*To* MAN.) … Did he say anything?

MAN
WIDOW

WIDOW   Did he say – did he say anything?

MAN

WIDOW   Did he / say –

BROTHER   (*To* GRANDDAD.) I don't want / to –

WIDOW   did he say / anything?

BROTHER   I don't want to know.

WIDOW   To you – did he – what did he (say)?

MAN
WIDOW

WIDOW   What did he say – to you? Did he – / what?

BROTHER   Tell her I don't / want to –

WIDOW   what did he say?

GRANDDAD   (*To* BROTHER.) Let her ask.

WIDOW   What did he say to / you?

25

BROTHER	Why does she want to / know?
WIDOW	I want to hear
BROTHER	why does she want / to hear?
GRANDDAD	Let her ask.
WIDOW	I want to hear / from –
GRANDDAD	Let her ask.
WIDOW	I want to hear from him.
BROTHER WIDOW	
WIDOW	From you.
MAN WIDOW	
WIDOW	What did he – did he / speak?
BROTHER	She doesn't have to –
GRANDDAD	it will help.
WIDOW	He spoke? He said / something?
BROTHER	It won't / help.
WIDOW	He would say something –
GRANDDAD	maybe it will / help.
WIDOW	What did he / *say*?
BROTHER	It won't help anything – she doesn't have / to –
WIDOW	Tell me.
	Beat.
GRANDDAD	… They say it could help / her.

BROTHER	Won't help me.
WIDOW	Tell me what he (said) – (*To* BROTHER.) this isn't about you –
BROTHER	this isn't about me – (*To* GRANDDAD.) is this helping / you?
WIDOW	Tell me what he said to you –
BROTHER	this isn't helping / you.
WIDOW	When he spoke – he / would –
BROTHER	and this isn't helping the / dead.
WIDOW	He would have spoken.

BROTHER *finds it hard to take.*

GRANDDAD	If you need to go –
BROTHER	I don't need to / go.
GRANDDAD	If you want to leave –
BROTHER	I'm not 'leaving' anywhere – you need a driver.
WIDOW	Did he say (anything) – did he say anything?
BROTHER	This is no / help.
WIDOW	Let me ask –
GRANDDAD	let her ask
WIDOW	let me / *speak*
BROTHER	I don't feel 'helped' –
WIDOW	he said / something?
BROTHER	(*To* GRANDDAD.) Do you feel 'helped'?
GRANDDAD	They said it would / hurt.
WIDOW	He would have said / something.

BROTHER	This much?
WIDOW	What did / he say?
GRANDDAD	Then help after that –
WIDOW	what did / he –
BROTHER	not after this – this is not / helping.
GRANDDAD	They said it could help her / after –
WIDOW	tell me if he – what / he –
BROTHER	this is not helping
WIDOW	did he / say anything?
BROTHER	This is not / helpful.
MAN	Do you want to know?

Beat.

Do you really want to know.

What he said.

Beat.

WIDOW	Yes.
GRANDDAD	… Yes.

Beat.

BROTHER	…
MAN	
BROTHER	
MAN	

Bosnia 1996

The two Serb MEN (*ex-soldiers*) *in civvies
are as they were.*
MAN 2 *moves to sit opposite* MAN 1.
BOSNIAN WOMAN *and* FRIEND *are not
there.*

MAN 2   … I have two kids.
A woman I go home to, at night.

Beat.

I work for my father-in-law.

MAN 1   No.

Beat.

MAN 2   My wife loves me and I love / her.

MAN 1   No.

MAN 2   My kids are school age – who I adore –

MAN 1   no.

MAN 2   My son has my spirit and my daughter lives
like her mother – laughs like her mother –
you are a single man – these are peaceful
times now

MAN 1   no

MAN 2   you are still a single man – you are not
employed

MAN 1   no

MAN 2   you are not employable – you drink you are
a drunk – if you say it was / you –

MAN 1	no
MAN 2	it won't matter – if you say it is yours
MAN 1	no
MAN 2	it doesn't matter. It doesn't matter.
MAN 2	
MAN 2	
MAN 2	I have two children. Eight and ten. A son and a daughter. A wife who waited for me a wife who I / adore.
MAN 1	No
MAN 2	a wife who I go home to – say it.
MAN 1	No.
MAN 2	I work for my father-in-law – say it
MAN 1	no
MAN 2	you don't work –
MAN 1	I don't / work.
MAN 2	You don't do anything
MAN 1	I don't do / anything.
MAN 2	You aren't anything – you were there
MAN 1	*you* were there
MAN 2	she remembers you.
MAN 1	She remembers *you*.

Beat.
Beat.

MAN 2 *awkwardly fingers his cigarette box, he draws a cigarette for himself but doesn't get round to lighting it as he speaks.*

MAN 2	…I have two / children –
MAN 1	you have 'two children'.
MAN 2	
MAN 2	You have / none.
MAN 1	You have a wife.
MAN 2	A wife who I –
MAN 1	'adore'.
MAN 2	
MAN 1	
MAN 2	You live life like a single / man.
MAN 1	I am a single man. You work for your father-in-law.
MAN 2	I work for my father-in-law –
MAN 1	you work for / your –
MAN 2	I work. You drink –
MAN 1	a lot
MAN 2	you could say the child – yes a lot – you could say the child is / yours –
MAN 1	I am a single / man.
MAN 2	her child is yours – you could say – you are – her child could be yours
MAN 1	could be / yours
MAN 2	you don't know it's not yours
MAN 1	neither do you.
MAN 2	…I served my country.
MAN 1	I served my / country.
MAN 2	*Just –*

MAN 2
MAN 1

MAN 2   …Just…
               Say… it.
               Then it won't matter.

               It won't matter.
               Really.

               Beat.

MAN 1   No.
               No.

Zimbabwe 2007

In another modest room, in another modest house. The Black ZIMBABWEAN HUSBAND *and* WIFE *sit and wait. They speak quietly.*

HUSBAND You who won't raise your voice – rose and spoke when you don't raise your voice to / me?

WIFE Why would I raise my voice to be heard in my own house?

HUSBAND This isn't our house

WIFE if this was our house.

HUSBAND This isn't our / home

WIFE when we were at home

HUSBAND we're not at / home

WIFE when we had a home – why would I raise my voice to / you there?

HUSBAND Not even a speech – not even a-a-a – long lecture –

WIFE it's not for me / to lecture.

HUSBAND Not a great oration – no standing ovation? No reasoning of the point – your point – no pros no / cons?

WIFE We're past the pros / and –

HUSBAND no slogans – no passionate performance –

WIFE I am not a performer.

33

HUSBAND	No rousing rhetoric?
WIFE	I am not a politician.
HUSBAND	No pause for the applause?
WIFE	There was no / applause.
HUSBAND	There was no applause?
WIFE	There was no applause.
HUSBAND	You got no applause from the 'few'? Nothing? You got nothing?

Beat.

WIFE	Someone clapping for me? I will not wait for that.
HUSBAND	You wait for nothing
WIFE	there is nothing worth waiting for.
HUSBAND	
HUSBAND	(*Dry.*) … Thank you.

They sit. They wait.

I'm all for / speaking –

WIFE	(*Quietly.*) no you're not
HUSBAND	I'm all for speaking up.
WIFE	No / you're –
HUSBAND	for speaking out
WIFE	no you're / not.
HUSBAND	If I was with you –
WIFE	you weren't with / me
HUSBAND	if I'd come with / you

WIFE	you didn't come with me – you don't come with me you'd stopped going and I won't wait for you to come I can't wait for you to never agree and I wasn't waiting for applause – I am just a woman –
HUSBAND	What?
WIFE	I am just a / woman.
HUSBAND	There are things that I would lose what we had for. There are things I wouldn't question to lose. There are things I would be proud to lose what we had for but for *this* – not even a speech – not even a sentence? To simply stand up and say –

There is a sharp, aggressive knocking from outside.
It makes them jump.

Silence.
They wait.
The knocking happens again.
Louder.

Rwanda 2005

> *The* MAN *sits opposite – as before.*
> GRANDDAD *is now sitting.*

WIDOW   … What was he wearing?
What was he – .

MAN

WIDOW   He was wearing some(thing) – what was /
he wearing?

GRANDDAD   (*To* BROTHER.) Tell her –

WIDOW   was he wearing / anything?

GRANDDAD   Tell her I don't need to / know –

WIDOW   when he was with you –

GRANDDAD   tell her I don't want / to –

WIDOW   when you were with / him.

GRANDDAD   I don't need to / know.

BROTHER   'Let her / ask.'

WIDOW   The last thing he had on – when I last saw
him the last thing he had on was –

GRANDDAD   I / can't –

WIDOW   his trousers were dark –

GRANDDAD   tell her I / can't –

WIDOW   the dark trousers he knew I didn't like –

GRANDDAD   I can't / know.

BROTHER	(*To* WIDOW.) Look / what –
GRANDDAD	I can't know any more.
WIDOW	I didn't like them and I said nothing.
BROTHER	(*To* WIDOW.) Look what this is / doing –
WIDOW	Just watched him wearing them – which made him… smile as he knew

GRANDDAD *is struggling.*

	he knew I knew he knew – that I didn't like them – even though I said nothing – his-his-his – top –
BROTHER	we don't / need –
WIDOW	his top / was –
GRANDDAD	we don't need to know – tell her I don't need / to know
WIDOW	was brand new second hand.
BROTHER	He doesn't need to know – we don't need to / know.
WIDOW	What he had on when I last saw him – when he was… when you had… what did he have / on?
GRANDDAD	(*To* BROTHER.) Tell her.
WIDOW	What did he have / on?
BROTHER	(*To* GRANDDAD.) You said –
WIDOW	I need to / hear.
BROTHER	you said to let her ask
GRANDDAD	why would you want to hear / that?
WIDOW	I need to hear from –

BROTHER	'let her ask'
GRANDDAD	why would she need to know that? I don't need to know / that.
WIDOW	I *want* to hear from him.
MAN WIDOW	
WIDOW	From that.
MAN WIDOW	
BROTHER	(*Dry.*) It could help –
GRANDDAD	won't help
BROTHER	no.
WIDOW	What did you see?
	When he was with / you.
GRANDDAD	This isn't helping me – this isn't about / me.
WIDOW	What did he have on?
BROTHER	(*To* MAN.) Just –
WIDOW	What was he / wearing –
GRANDDAD	tell her I can't –
BROTHER	(*To* MAN.) just / tell –
WIDOW	when you had / him –
BROTHER	(*To* MAN.) just tell her
GRANDDAD	I can't hear – tell her – I don't want to / hear
WIDOW	when he left us he / was –
BROTHER	tell / her

GRANDDAD	this is / no help
BROTHER	*tell her*
WIDOW	*tell me* – he had on – what?
GRANDDAD	Tell her to / stop –
WIDOW	When he was with / you –
GRANDDAD	tell her / to stop
WIDOW	when you had him – *what was / he wearing*?
MAN	Do you want to know?

Beat.
Beat.

Do you want to know?

WIDOW	Yes.

Beat.

MAN	What he was wearing?

Beat.

BROTHER	… … Yes.
MAN	Really?

GRANDDAD *starts to quietly cry.*

South Africa 1998

> NANA, SON *and* DAUGHTER *are seated as before, still waiting.* MAMA *still standing. The chair opposite them remains empty.*
>
> *Beat.*
> *Beat.*

DAUGHTER

SON

NANA

> *Beat.*
> DAUGHTER *very quietly half-sings/hums part of a broken protest song, bored.*

NANA   Tell your mama... to sit.

DAUGHTER

NANA   Tell your mama to (sit) ...

SON
DAUGHTER

> DAUGHTER *makes no attempt to move.*
> SON *gets up.*

SON   Mama –

NANA   tell your mama to...
               sit down here...
               by me.

MAMA

> DAUGHTER *breaks from her half-song.*

DAUGHTER   Mama – .

NANA	I am askin you… to sit… on one of these hard chairs.
	By me. Daughter.
	MAMA *doesn't move.* SON *isn't sure what* *to do.*
	Tell your mama I want her to sit –
DAUGHTER	Mama –
NANA	side by side with / me.
SON	Mama.
NANA	Tell your mama I… need her to sit side by side with / me.
MAMA	I have no body to bury.
	I have had no body to bury.
NANA	Daughter – please – sit / down.
MAMA	I have twenty-two years of not knowing to wonder on. And live with. With no body to bury. They have had twenty-two years knowing. And not saying. *Twenty-two.*
	Knowing how they took her from me. When

they took her from me
and the luxury
of living with the knowledge
of knowing that.
They have had that.

They have their last look
at her.
Which was later than mine.
Their last words with her.
Which were after mine.
The last words she heard...

That were not mine.

What I have had to imagine.
They know.
And have known.
And have left me to
my merciless
imagination.
For –
twenty-two
years.

And now...
they don't even bother
they won't even bother
to say

after twenty-two years
that they will not come.

That they cannot be
bothered
to turn up.
That they cannot be
bothered
to sit opposite me
and face me

and tell me
twenty-two years
later
what… happened. To my firstborn.
What they did to my firstborn.

They are…

shameless.

That I still have
no body.
To bury.
No remains
to put to rest.
To put me at rest.
No answer.

No answers.
Twenty-two years later.

They
let me stand here
to look at
an empty chair
opposite me.
They leave me to
look at that?
No Mama. *No* Mama.
I will not…

sit down.
I will not
sit
on an empty hard chair
on any
empty hard chair.

By you
or by
myself.

Not before
one of
them

sits down
in front of me

on their hard chair

first.

Northern Ireland 1999

> *The* WOMAN *is standing, a bit agitated. The others sit in the three chairs. Two* MEN, *and another* WOMAN (A). *The empty chair and* WOMAN, *opposite them. They watch her.*

MAN A   … Take a seat –

WOMAN   huh?

MAN A   Why don'tchu take the weight off so / we can –

WOMAN   you think I need to – so you think I need to? You're presuming / I need to.

MAN A   It's easier / to –

MAN B   I'm not going to sit here and look up at you – tell her I'm not going to sit here and look up at her – sit down so we can all have a – tell her to sit down so we can all / have a –

WOMAN   why don't you stand then, big man. Tell him to get up if sitting is such a problem. Or you're asking me to sit so you can feel better? So he can feel better – is that what you're saying? Is this what he's like love? Is this what he's saying? Is this how he is / with you?

WOMAN A   I'm not / your 'love'.

WOMAN   Demanding you do what he wants for his convenience?

MAN B
WOMAN

45

WOMAN	This is nothing about me taking the weight off. It's all about you… watching me at your level.
MAN B	I'm not at your level believe / me.
WOMAN	Presuming.
MAN B	Tell her, I'm not at her level – I wouldn't sink to somewhere so / low as –
MAN A	(*To* MAN B.) we're not / here for that
MAN B	as to comprehend what low-life level she / lives on.
WOMAN	'She'?
MAN B	You.
MAN A	We've not come for that now, come / on.
WOMAN	Showing your true colours – showing his true colours now love – is / this what –
WOMAN A	I'm not / your 'love'.
WOMAN	is this what he's truly like behind closed doors? Is this what you're (like)? – others may jump when you say boo – she may jump when you say so but I'm not moving.

She watches MAN B.

	Can hardly keep it contained – he can hardly keep it contained – can you – can't suit it and boot it dress it up any different than it is – than you are cos as soon as you open your mouth – as soon as he opens his mouth he exposes himself – you expose yourself – you're sitting in the wrong seat maybe you're sitting in the – maybe he's sitting in the wrong seat love –
WOMAN A	I'm not / your 'love'.

46

WOMAN	you tell him that.
MAN B	
WOMAN	
WOMAN	Tell him something cos he needs telling. He needs someone to tell him something about himself.
MAN A	C'mon now c'mon.
	MAN B *watches her*.
WOMAN	Or isn't she allowed.

Rwanda 2005

> *The* MAN *sits opposite – as before.*
> WIDOW *is seated.*

WIDOW   Was he…?

BROTHER   Stop.

> *Beat.*

WIDOW   Was he crying –

BROTHER   (*To* WIDOW.) Stop.

WIDOW   Was he crying when he / was –

GRANDDAD   stop / her

WIDOW   was he crying when he was with you?

> *Beat.*

GRANDDAD   We don't want to know –

BROTHER   I told you. (*To* WIDOW.) You don't need to
               / know.

WIDOW   Did you make him / cry?

GRANDDAD   Tell her – stop / her.

BROTHER   (*To* GRANDDAD.) I've told her.

WIDOW   Did you make him / cry?

GRANDDAD   She doesn't listen to / me.

WIDOW   Did / you?

GRANDDAD   Stop her

WIDOW   did *you* / make him –

BROTHER   she won't listen to / me

WIDOW	did you force him to – was he – was he – *was / he* – ?
BROTHER	(*To* WIDOW.) *Stop / now.*
GRANDDAD	Stop her –
BROTHER	you need to stop
WIDOW	tell him I have to hear – if you need to leave
BROTHER	you need to stop – and I need to 'leave' / nowhere.
WIDOW	I 'need' –
GRANDDAD	you 'need' to finish / now.
WIDOW	I could have come on my own – I should have come on my own – I 'need' to hear if / he –
GRANDDAD	why? Ask her why?
WIDOW	Was he crying?
GRANDDAD	Stop her – as his brother –
WIDOW	was he – ?
BROTHER	You are his father
WIDOW	was / he?
GRANDDAD	You can stop her –
WIDOW	I am his *wife* –
GRANDDAD	as a man as a man stop / her –
WIDOW	*was / he?*
GRANDDAD	*Stop her!* This is not helping.

BROTHER *tries to physically stop*
WIDOW, *gently at first, she resists, his grip
is firm, she starts to physically fight to stay.*

WIDOW   Let *me* speak – let *me* ask – let / me –

               As BROTHER *and* WIDOW *continue*
               physically struggling with each other.

MAN   (*Dry.*) They said it would help…

               BROTHER *lets his grip on* WIDOW *go.*
               He squares up to the MAN. *The* MAN
               doesn't flinch.

Zimbabwe 2007

Three wooden chairs facing one solitary wooden chair. Black ZIMBABWEAN HUSBAND *is seated in one of the three chairs.*
Black ZIMBABWEAN WOMAN (*not his* WIFE), *standing.*

WOMAN   … The fact that you…

She watches him.

The fact that you –

HUSBAND   the / 'fact'?

WOMAN   The fact that you are here sitting / there.

HUSBAND   The 'facts' –

WOMAN   says to me –

HUSBAND   the 'facts' to you – you stand there and talk of 'facts' / to me?

WOMAN   it says to me you have already / made up your –

HUSBAND   The 'facts' to / you.

WOMAN   that you have already made up your mind – your mind is already made / up of –

HUSBAND   What *you* think –

WOMAN   'what I think'

HUSBAND   what you think means nothing to me.

WOMAN   I / think –

51

HUSBAND	what you / think –
WOMAN	I think the 'fact' that you sit there – over / there –
HUSBAND	is nothing – what you / know –
WOMAN	over there mind made up says something.
HUSBAND	What you know is what I need / to –
WOMAN	'Need' now?
HUSBAND	… 'Want' to – find / out.
WOMAN	And sitting there in those seats on that side says something. Is saying something. Before I even speak. Says something about your… need eh? That I'm expected to be seated here. You expect me to sit here? You expect me to sit here. I won't. I should be sitting there with you – I should be (there) – because I will not sit down – I will *not* sit down I will not sit down in this seat on this side… saying something sinister – it says something sinister before I've even spoken. No. Others may accept that – shit – and sit there. Others may have done things for them to sit there. Who has sat in this seat before me – who is coming after me? I am not them that I should be sitting / over there.
HUSBAND	She / is –
WOMAN	The '*fact*' is – as I have told / you –
HUSBAND	she is / my –

WOMAN	is that I don't know – I wouldn't know – I / didn't know –
HUSBAND	the fact is she is my wife.

Beat.

WOMAN	You raise your voice to me? … You raise your voice to me? I wasn't there.
HUSBAND	You didn't have / to be (there).
WOMAN	I didn't see / her –
HUSBAND	you didn't need to see her you know / that.
WOMAN	I / didn't –
HUSBAND	Everybody knows / that.
WOMAN	I didn't do –
HUSBAND	what?
WOMAN HUSBAND	
WOMAN	To her. Nothing. To her.

I will not stay standing… to have you
accuse (me)…
And I will not sit there
and be accused.

She moves a chair.

… The people you want are those that took
her.
The people who should be in here – who
should be sitting there – over there are…
should be the ones that took / her.

HUSBAND	Who / ordered –

WOMAN	The people you should be questioning are those that knocked on / your –
HUSBAND	who ordered your / men?
WOMAN	knocked on your door –
HUSBAND	Who ordered them to take / her?
WOMAN	which wasn't me. I took no one.
HUSBAND	Who ordered them to take her?
WOMAN	I didn't knock your door. Did I knock your door? I didn't knock on your (door) – it wasn't even your door. How could I take anyone – look at me.

Beat.

I am… just a woman. Who am I to order anyone?

HUSBAND	You were at the / meeting.
WOMAN	Who am I to order men? What man would take an order from a woman? From this woman?

HUSBAND	
WOMAN	

WOMAN	What kind of man would that be? If a man wants to take orders from a woman… then maybe he deserves to be seated there – did you take orders from your wife? Would you take orders from your / wife?
HUSBAND	I am her / husband.
WOMAN	Did she give you orders…? Are you that kind of… man? Was it that kind of – 'marriage'? Or did you raise your voice to her as well?

She watches him.

(*Dry.*) I don't think / so.

HUSBAND   I am her husband. She is –

WOMAN   was.
Fact.

HUSBAND
WOMAN

HUSBAND   ... My wife.

Beat.

WOMAN   ... You should control your woman.

HUSBAND

WOMAN   Maybe you should have controlled your
woman's mouth. Maybe you should have
raised your voice to control your woman's
mouth. I recommend / it.

HUSBAND   Is / she –

WOMAN   What kind of man doesn't know where his
woman is?
Doesn't know what his woman is doing?
Doesn't know what his woman is saying?
Was saying.

HUSBAND
WOMAN

WOMAN   What kind of man doesn't / care?

HUSBAND   Is she / still –

WOMAN   What kind of man is that?
What kind of husband is that?
What kind of man are / you?

HUSBAND   Is she still alive?

WOMAN   Nobody persuaded her.

	Nobody applauded her. Nobody asked her to stand up and speak.
HUSBAND	Is she still alive?
WOMAN	You ask me… expecting me to know. Expecting me to answer. Expecting an answer.
HUSBAND WOMAN	
WOMAN	How will – you – make me answer? How will someone like you… make someone like me answer a question from – someone like you?
HUSBAND	
WOMAN	Raise your voice.
HUSBAND	
WOMAN	… My husband knows where I am. My husband knows what I do. Your faulty family structure is… your fault.
HUSBAND	Is she still / alive?
WOMAN	Whatever happened to your woman – your wife – is partly down to you.
HUSBAND	Is she still alive?
WOMAN	So. That seat there. Therefore. Will not be mine.

Beat.

*She gestures for him to take the solo seat
opposite her.*

He does not move.

Rwanda 2005

> *The* MAN *and the* WIDOW *remain.*
> BROTHER *and* GRANDDAD *have left.*
> *Their seats are empty.*

MAN
WIDOW

MAN   What else?
             What else do you want to know…?

             Beat.

             What else do you want me to / say?

WIDOW   That you remember him.

             Beat.

             He was memorable.

MAN
MAN

WIDOW   He was / memorable.

MAN   There were a few –

WIDOW   you would remember him.

MAN
WIDOW

MAN   … He was one of… of a / few.

WIDOW   Tell me that you remember him.

WIDOW

WIDOW   You would remember him – .

MAN

WIDOW	He's not someone to forget –
MAN	for you.
WIDOW	
MAN	
MAN	… Some of –
WIDOW	yes?
MAN	Some of them –
WIDOW	yes?
MAN	Your / one –
WIDOW	*yes?*
WIDOW	
MAN	
MAN	… He said you –
WIDOW	what?
MAN	He / said –
WIDOW	*what?*
MAN	
WIDOW	
MAN	He said… he was ashamed to beg – be begging. When he was begging. He said… he said it was something you wouldn't do.
WIDOW	
MAN	Your one – he was ashamed to cry – be crying. When he was crying. He said it was something you wouldn't do.
WIDOW	This is / not –

MAN	he was ashamed when he vomited –
WIDOW	this is one of your 'others' –
MAN	said you wouldn't / do that–
WIDOW	not him – this is not him – this is one of your 'a / few' –
MAN	your one – was ashamed when he shit / his self –
WIDOW	no
MAN	he was memorable
WIDOW	no
MAN	in his funny dark trousers – I didn't like them either. He was…

Beat.

WIDOW	… What?
MAN	Tormented… by you.
WIDOW	
MAN	By not being how you are and being how weak he is –
WIDOW	you / can –
MAN	how weak he – was.
WIDOW	This is not him – you can / stop.
MAN	He called you.
WIDOW	You can stop / now.
MAN	He called for you –
WIDOW	stop / now
MAN	he called your name
WIDOW	this is not him –

MAN	he called –
WIDOW	this is not / *him*
MAN	he called your –
WIDOW	no.
MAN	Stella… Stella.
WIDOW	
WIDOW	
MAN	Before.
	During…
	In his horrible trousers.
WIDOW	
MAN	
MAN	Stella.
	I see – Stella…
	That… you have in you
	the capacity to do to me.
	What I did to him.
	And you have in you… Stella
	the ability
	like me.
	To live with it.
WIDOW	
MAN	

Northern Ireland 1999

> *ALL are seated. The* WOMAN *digs in her handbag for her pack of cigarettes.*

WOMAN   You can sit there and watch me all you like I'm only sitting cos I'm sick of standing if I knew I'd be standing for hours I would've worn different shoes – worn better shoes – flats – d'you have a light?

MAN A
WOMAN
MAN B
WOMAN

WOMAN   (Don't be) looking at me like that – looking at me like that all you want – lookin at me like you're all some non-smoking angels when I know you've still a fondness for the nicotine Shane and still walk with a light so stop being something you're not and offer it / up.

WOMAN A   There's no smoking in here.

WOMAN   Someone say something?

MAN B   She said there is no smoking in / here.

WOMAN   She allowed to speak or are you speaking for her – again?

> *No one offers her a light. She puts her cigarette away.*
> *Beat.*

… Well.

	Beat.
MAN A	Well.
	Beat.
WOMAN	Who to go first.
	Beat.
MAN A	… It's not us with something to say.
WOMAN	I have nothing to say –
MAN B	you / do.
WOMAN	Nothing to apologise for –
MAN B	she does
MAN A	you do
WOMAN A	you do.
WOMAN WOMAN A	
	Beat. *A silence.*
WOMAN A	… Nothing to say?
WOMAN	
WOMAN A	Not sayin nothin. A habit with / you.
WOMAN	Habit?
WOMAN A	A habit with / you.
MAN B	A habit with / her –
WOMAN	(*To* WOMAN A.) You know nothin about me… You know *nothin* about – any habits that I haven't the luxury for. I don't have the luxury for habits, for any habits – I don't

have 'habits' – but you wouldn't know
about that. Love.
Would / you?

WOMAN A   I'm not your love

MAN B   don't let her get under / your –

WOMAN A   she's not she just –

MAN B   it's what she / does.

WOMAN   Do you want us to leave the room or can we
all watch this little domestic?

WOMAN A   … You're not as… as you think you are.

WOMAN   … Y'know what?
I think I am.

WOMAN A   If you have something to say –

MAN B   you have something to say – she has
something to / say.

MAN A   She has something to / say.

WOMAN A   Just say it. For / once.

WOMAN   I need no one's permission to say anything
– I don't need your permission to say
anything – not been waiting for you to give
me permission – not waiting for your say-
so to say something – from the woman who
wouldn't know what truth was if it came
and slapped you round that loose mouth of /
yours.

MAN B *is agitated.*

MAN B   Alright – this is just / getting us (nowhere).

WOMAN A   It's alright it's / alright –

MAN A   it's / alright –

WOMAN A	listen – I can –
MAN A	she can – she's / fine
WOMAN A	I can (do this) – sit down. *Sit down*.

MAN B *re-sits*.
WOMAN *watches them both*.

MAN B	I'm not having her speeching I'm not / having –
MAN A	we're not here for speeches
WOMAN	I'm not speechin I'm just sayin.
WOMAN A	So say somethin then.
WOMAN	Says you.
WOMAN A	She makes me / feel –
WOMAN	'She'?
WOMAN A	*You* – make me feel – she makes me feel – she makes a woman feel ill.
WOMAN	You couldn't make me feel anything.
WOMAN A	I haven't done anything
WOMAN	you think? Sitting there presuming what about me? I haven't done anything. I haven't done anything / wrong.
MAN B	All she had to do – all you had to do / was –
WOMAN A	no let / me –
MAN B	all / she –
MAN A	I know
WOMAN A	let me.
WOMAN	(*Dry*.) Yes let her

WOMAN A	*don't*.
WOMAN	Or what? 'Don't' what? A threat? From you?
WOMAN WOMAN A	
WOMAN	Fuckin… laughable.
WOMAN A	You said… nothing. You said – *nothin* –
WOMAN	You know nothing about my 'nothings' –
WOMAN A	You're choosing to say / nothing.
WOMAN	you know *nothing* about my-my-my-and-and – 'choosing'? Choices? 'Habits'? Your definitions are for you – I had no / choice.
WOMAN A	He was my son.
WOMAN	What about my son?
WOMAN A	Fuck your son.
WOMAN	Fuck you –
WOMAN A	says the woman who bred the fucking beast –
WOMAN	fucking / 'beast'?
WOMAN A	Your son was the fucking / problem.
WOMAN	Fucking 'beast'?! Bold now aren'tcha – bold now / aren'tcha?
WOMAN A	Down to a level of language that you'll / understand.
WOMAN	Been taking tips from tin-man here? What – he (*Meaning* MAN B.) had a word – bolstered you up giving you the bollocks to

talk to me like that – who the fuck d'you think you're talking / to?

WOMAN A   Who the fuck do you think you are?

WOMAN
WOMAN A

WOMAN   She can cut me – you can cut me down for what I do say but she can't sit there and criticise me for what I / didn't.

WOMAN A   What you don't say loses lives.

WOMAN   She doesn't know that –

WOMAN A   I'm *telling you* / that.

MAN A   You knew what your boy was going to / do.

WOMAN   Did / I?

WOMAN A   And what he did was unforgiveable and you're unforgiveable for not saying something sooner that could have stopped / it.

WOMAN   Your boy had a mind of his own –

WOMAN A   not after your fucker whispered in / it.

MAN A   You knew what your boy was going / to do.

WOMAN   Or was his mind as weak as his mother's?

WOMAN A   I raised my son –

WOMAN   I raised my son –

WOMAN A   not to lose him to yours's fuckin cause.

MAN B   She knew what her boy was going / to do –

WOMAN A   what she doesn't say loses lives – toldju –

MAN B   I / know.

WOMAN   I came / here –

WOMAN A	What she doesn't *do* loses / lives –
MAN B	I / know.
WOMAN	I came here – on my own – that's what kind of woman / I am.
WOMAN A	You could've / stopped it.
WOMAN	That I came here at all – is what kind of woman / I am.
WOMAN A	She could've stopped / him.
MAN A	You could've / stopped him.
WOMAN A	And saved a lot of mourning mothers in the meantime.
WOMAN	I'm a mother in mourning –
WOMAN A	your own fault.
WOMAN	… I've been mannersable and polite and put up with all your three-to-one bollocks trying to batter me – but that's the kind of woman I am. You turn up with your bullshit back-up –
MAN B	I'm no / back-up –
WOMAN	with your mock-up muscle –
MAN A	it's not like / that
WOMAN	sit there and try and play / coy –
MAN A	it's not like / that.
MAN B	I'm no / back-up.
WOMAN	Think you're something that you're not and say nothing without permission. What kind of woman are you? What kind of mother were you?
WOMAN A	What kind of mother were / *you*?

| WOMAN | I stand up and say somethin back then – then what? What? Don't – don't tell me about choice – don't *tell* me about choices – don't sit there and say to me about – I won't fuckin –
Don't. |
|---|---|
| WOMAN A | |
| WOMAN | |
| WOMAN | … And I'll take that light off you Shane now. If you don't mind.

Beat.
Beat.
Pause. |

Rwanda 2005

The MAN *is exhausted.*
MOSES (*Stella's husband*) *watches him.*
MOSES *is dead.*

MOSES … What is it you want to know?
What else do you want to know?

Beat.

What do you want to ask? Ask.

Did it hurt?
… Yes. It hurt.

MAN It hurts

MOSES it does.

MAN
MAN

MAN … I have seen –

MOSES did I ask you what you have seen?

MAN

MAN … Things that are not meant to be (seen) – I
have done –

MOSES did I ask you what you have done?

MAN … Things that I know / have –

MOSES Did you hear me asking – when did you
hear me ask? Do you hear me asking to
know – no.
I don't care. I do not care.
I do not care for regrets – I do not care for

70

	your regrets. I do not care for – your slippery words keep them – I can't be bothered with your… ruefulness – can't be bothered with that reconciliatory bullshit. Keep it. I am not looking to be reconciled.
MAN	
MOSES	
MAN	
MAN	I don't sleep
MOSES	good.
MAN	I have no appetite.
MOSES	Good.
MAN	Drink doesn't get me drunk. I stay sober –
MOSES	good.
MAN	People are afraid of / me –
MOSES	that you never have a night's sleep again – would be too soon.
MAN	
MOSES	Yes.
MAN	My friends are afraid of / me.
MOSES	That your laughter will always ring hollow…
	MOSES *nods*.
	Yes.
MAN	I have no friends –
MOSES	good.
MAN	I keep no / friends –
MOSES	good.

MAN	I keep no / company.
MOSES	That your eyes will close and that you will see me that you will turn over for respite and remember me that you will think one time, one night's sleep is coming – that there will be relief but… no. It will be me. Sleep will be a memory / for you.
MAN	My family fear / me.
MOSES	You fucking *fuck*.
MAN	… My mother pretends / with me.
MOSES	We are not honourable dead
MAN	she is glad when I'm / gone
MOSES	we are not reflective and / forgiving
MAN	my father is always / out
MOSES	we are not forgiving
MAN	out when I am in.
MOSES	We are not forgiving you – I am not forgiving / you
MAN	so I don't stay in.
MOSES	We are not the glorious dead. There is nothing glorious about us. About me. You fuck. *Beat.*
MAN	… I drink till I am sick but my head stays / clear.

MOSES	We are just… bitter bodies.
MAN	… I came / here –
MOSES	how is / my wife?
MAN	I came / here.
MOSES	How is my wife?
	Beat.
MAN	I came here –
MOSES	you have said – now I am asking. How is my Stella?
MAN	I… I…
MOSES MAN	
MOSES	You will know her by the amount of questions she will ask. She will ask you a million questions – at a million miles an hour. She will not stop. She is unstoppable. She does not drive but she will be there. She is unmistakeable. That is my woman.
	You like these trousers?
MAN	
MOSES	You like these trousers?
MAN	Yes.
MOSES	She does not. I know she knows I know. That is my woman.

MAN	
MOSES	You will handle her fairly.
MAN	
MOSES	You will put her at ease.
	You will tell her the truth. How I fought you how fiercely I fought you. How you struggled with me how I scarred you how you had to call for help to finish what you / started
MAN	you / were –
MOSES	because you couldn't kill / me
MAN	you were the first one that / I –
MOSES	you couldn't even kill me on your own. You will tell her that truth.
MAN	
MOSES	So. How is my wife? How is my Stella? What did she say? What did she say? Eh?

South Africa 1976

> *The Black* CHILD *(female), approx*
> *fourteen, sees the chairs. The* CHILD *is*
> *dead.*
> *A white* SOUTH AFRICAN POLICE
> OFFICER *in uniform is standing.*
> *The* CHILD *watches the* OFFICER *sit on*
> *the row of three.*
> *The* CHILD *moves the spare chairs over to*
> *the other side. The* OFFICER *is now in a*
> *solo chair with three facing him.*

CHILD   (*Carefree*.) When you pushed me I thought
it was an accident –

OFFICER   it wasn't a push

CHILD   I thought it was / accidental

OFFICER   it wasn't a push it was a knock.

> *Beat.*

CHILD   You were in a hurry –

OFFICER   everyone was in a / hurry.

CHILD   I was running.

OFFICER   Everyone was running.

CHILD   I was running away.

OFFICER

CHILD   When you held me I thought it was by
mistake – that you thought you were
holding someone / else.

OFFICER	I didn't know you
CHILD	that you thought I was someone else –
OFFICER	I didn't need to know / you
CHILD	when you pulled me to my feet I thought you had realised that I wasn't the someone else you were looking for.
OFFICER	
CHILD	That when you saw me you would let me go.
OFFICER	
CHILD	But when you held me – kept holding me from behind and wouldn't let me look – at you – I didn't know how you would know you didn't know me if you wouldn't let me turn around and see your face.
OFFICER	… I didn't want to see your / face.
CHILD	I couldn't see your face – I didn't know how you would – how would you know I wasn't who you were looking / for?
OFFICER	I wasn't looking for someone. I was looking for anyone.
	Beat.
CHILD	When I tried to turn around and you slapped my face / forward –
OFFICER	don't turn / around
CHILD	I didn't know what to / do.
OFFICER	Don't turn around.
CHILD	I didn't know what to do what I should do – when I started crying and couldn't stop – I couldn't stop –

OFFICER	I couldn't / stop.
CHILD	I couldn't stop and couldn't stop shaking and when you started shouting
OFFICER	I asked you to / stop
CHILD	when you shouted I just shook some more.
OFFICER	
CHILD	I heard the draw back.
OFFICER	No you / didn't.
CHILD	I heard the draw back
OFFICER	you couldn't have / heard.
CHILD	Among all the shouting and running and bangs and cars and trucks and people I heard the draw back metal on / metal.
OFFICER	Then it wasn't my draw back that you heard it wasn't / mine –
CHILD	what happened to rubber bullets? What happened to rubber bullets first? What happened to rubber bullets first fired in the air and verbal warnings – what happened to / that?
OFFICER	There was a warning –
CHILD	there was no warning
OFFICER	there was a verbal / warning
CHILD	there was no verbal / warning.
OFFICER	I was shouting
CHILD	that was not a warning. That was not the warning. There was no warning.
OFFICER	

OFFICER	… There was no / warning.
CHILD	What happened to rubber bullets?
OFFICER	
CHILD	Live rounds with no warning?
OFFICER	
CHILD	When you shot me my eardrum blew first. Loud.
OFFICER	
CHILD	It was loud – you were close.
OFFICER	You wouldn't stand still.
CHILD	I was shaking
OFFICER	you were running
CHILD	I was running away. Everyone was running away.

CHILD (cont.)

I counted sixteen.
Live rounds.
From you.
Amongst the other
live rounds
around me.

My stones
were no match.

OFFICER	
CHILD	I counted sixteen fired, four hit – from you – the first killed me – the extra – weren't you sure?
OFFICER	I / didn't –
CHILD	sixteen?
OFFICER	I didn't – I don't leave wounded / I –

78

CHILD	you should've known after the first – I fell / after the first.
OFFICER	you were still shaking.
CHILD	I fell after the first – by the B of the bang I was deaf. By the G of the bang I was / dead.
OFFICER	You were still shaking you were still shaking you were still shaking... You were.
OFFICER CHILD	
OFFICER	You / were.
CHILD	Twenty-two years from now you will sit opposite my mama my nana my brother and my sister... You will tell them about your... live rounds. You will tell them about your sixteen fired with no warning. You will tell them what happened. To me. What you did to me. Where what is left of me is. Now. You will let them find me.

OFFICER
CHILD

CHILD   What is left of me.
                    Where you and your –
                    colleagues
                    dumped me.

                    You will show them.
                    And you will tell them.
                    Tell my mama.
                    And she will not sit.
                    And she will not cry.

                    And she is as strong as she looks.
                    Stronger than you.

                    And my nana will not be impressed
                    by these…
                    hard chairs.

                    But you will tell them.

                    You will go.
                    You will go.

                    You will not be late.
                    You will not be willing.
                    But you will go.

                    And you will tell them.

OFFICER
CHILD

OFFICER   …Ja.

                    I will go.

                    End.

A Nick Hern Book

truth and reconciliation first published in Great Britain in 2011 as a paperback original by Nick Hern Books Limited, 14 Larden Road, London W3 7ST, in association with the Royal Court Theatre, London

Cover image: Matthew Hollings
Cover design: Ned Hoste, 2H

Typeset by Nick Hern Books, London
Printed in the UK by CPI Group (UK) Ltd, Croydon, CR0 4YY

A CIP catalogue record for this book is available from the British Library

ISBN 978 1 84842 172 1